BE NOT AFRAID

Pope John Paul II's Words of

Faith, Hope, and Love

9   8   7   6   5   4   3   2   1
Digit on the right indicates the number of this printing

Library of Congress Control Number: 2005929944
ISBN-13: 978-0-7624-2642-3
ISBN-10: 0-7624-2642-X

Cover and interior design by Susan Van Horn
Quotes compiled by MaryAnn Gardner

Photography research by Susan Oyama
Typography: Centaur, Poetica Chancery and Serlio

This book may be ordered by mail from the publisher.
But try your bookstore first!

Published by Courage Books, an imprint of
Running Press Book Publishers
125 South Twenty-second Street
Philadelphia, Pennsylvania 19103-4399

Visit us on the web!
www.runningpress.com

BE NOT AFRAID

Pope John Paul II's Words of
Faith, Hope, and Love

Introduction by Archbishop John P. Foley
President of the Pontifical Council for Social Communications

Edited by Diana C. von Glahn

COURAGE BOOKS
AN IMPRINT OF RUNNING PRESS
PHILADELPHIA • LONDON

CONTENTS

———◆———

Pope John Paul II at Castel Gandolfo during his first official
public appearance as pope. (Italy; October 25, 1978)

Introduction

Pope John Paul II once told me that he realized the importance of symbols during his public encounters.

"I don't plan them," he said. "They are spontaneous. . . . But, as you know, the word *symbol* comes from the Greek word *symbolein*—to bring together; it is the opposite of the Greek word *diabolein*—to break apart—the origin of our words *devil* and *diabolical*."

Symbolic actions, the Holy Father pointed out, should unite people in understanding and love. This beautiful book, *Be Not Afraid*, which takes its title from the opening words of Pope John Paul's inaugural homily in 1978, shows through magnificent photos the power of those symbolic actions. It also recalls the timeless teachings of this great pontiff on the themes of Faith, Hope, and Love.

Those who wish a lasting reminder of the striking images and moving words of the late and great Pope John Paul II to give them courage and consolation will find a pleasant companion in *Be Not Afraid*.

—Archbishop John P. Foley

President of the Pontifical Council for Social Communications

PREFACE

"So faith, hope, love abide, these three; but the greatest of these is love."

I am a proud member of the JPII Generation. Although Karol Wojtyla became Pope John Paul II seven years after I was born, he was, until recently, the only Holy Father I'd ever really known.

John Paul II was many things for many people, but for me and for many of my generation, he was *Papa*, always teaching, always guiding toward holiness, toward Christ. "Papa", the Italian word for "pope", captures the role that the Holy Father took as Vicar of Christ. Like an earthly father, he led his spiritual children toward truth with a firm, yet loving hand, challenging us to become the best Christians we could be.

There is a great deal that can and has been said about Pope John Paul II. *Be Not Afraid* speaks to us with the words the Holy Father used himself. These words, and those of his many writings, call us to persist in our faith, give us hope for the future, and courage to love despite adversity. They compel us to recall the words of St. Paul who, in 1 Corinthians 13, reminds us that without love, we are nothing.

May this book inspire you in the way it has me, may it motivate you to seek out the Holy Father's writings, and encourage you to cultivate the virtues of faith, hope, and love.

—The Editor

FAITH

No treasure is as uplifting and
transforming as the light of faith.

—St. Patrick's Cathedral, New York, October 7, 1995

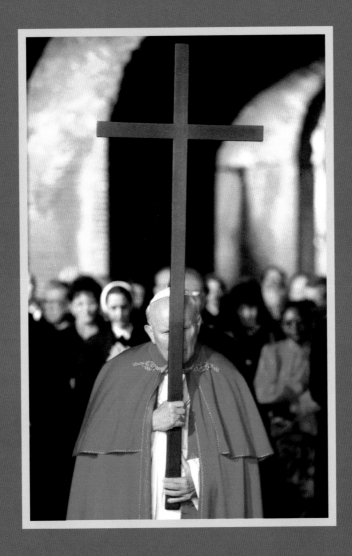

The Holy Father leads pilgrims around Rome's Colisseum during the Good Friday procession of the *Via Crucis* (Way of the Cross). Pope John Paul II led this procession every year during his 27-year pontificate until his last year when he was too ill. (April 5, 1996)

For his seventh foreign Apostolic trip, the Pope visited Brazil.
He was met with shouts of joy and showers of confetti. (1980)

There is a temptation which perennially besets every spiritual journey and pastoral work: that of thinking that the results depend on our ability to act and to plan. God of course asks us really to cooperate with his grace, and therefore invites us to invest all our resources of intelligence and energy in serving the cause of the Kingdom. But it is fatal to forget that "without Christ we can do nothing."

—*Novo Millennio Ineunte*, January 6, 2001

In the far reaches of the human heart there
is a seed of desire and nostalgia for God....
There is therefore a path which the human
being may choose to take, a path which begins
with reason's capacity to rise beyond what is
contingent and set out toward the infinite.

—*Fides et Ratio*, September 14, 1998

The Pope walks through Lithuania's Hill of Crosses during his first
trip to the countries of the former Soviet Union. More than 50,000
crosses cover the hill to commemorate the many who lost their lives
rebelling against more than a century of Russian and Communist
oppression. (Siauliai, Lithuania; September 7, 1993)

Pope John Paul II raises a monstrance that contains the Blessed Sacrament during a ceremony in St. Peter's Square marking the start of the International Eucharist conference, one of the highlights of the Jubilee year. (Vatican City, June 19, 2000)

Even when it is celebrated on the humble altar of a country church, the Eucharist is always in some way celebrated on the altar of the world. It unites heaven and earth. It embraces and permeates all creation. The Son of God became man in order to restore all creation, in one supreme act of praise, to the One who made it from nothing. . . . Truly this is the *mysterium fidei* which is accomplished in the Eucharist: the world which came forth from the hands of God the Creator now returns to him redeemed by Christ.

—*Ecclesia de Eucharistia*, April 17, 2003

[P]rayer is not a kind of delegating to the
Lord so that he can act in our place.
Instead it is confiding in him, putting
ourselves in his hands, which makes us
in turn confident and ready to do God's work.

—To the Clergy of Rome, February 14, 2002

⸻ ✛ ⸻

GIVE SIGNIFICANT TIME TO PRAYER, TO LISTENING

TO GOD'S WORD AND TO CHRISTIAN EDUCATION;

IN THEM YOU WILL FIND EFFECTIVE SUPPORT TO TACKLE

THE DIFFICULTIES OF DAILY LIFE AND

THE GREAT CHALLENGES OF TODAY'S WORLD.

—Homily at the Abbassyin Stadium of Damascus, May 6, 2001

The Pope prays before the relics of St. Remigius in Reims' St. Remi Basilica. (France; September 22, 1996)

Pope John Paul II delivers his *Urbi et Orbi* (Latin for "To the City and the World") blessing from the central balcony of St. Peter's Basilica during Easter Sunday celebrations. The *Urbi et Orbi* messages are generally delivered on Easter and Christmas. (Vatican City; April 7, 1996)

The call of the Lord Jesus "You too go into my vineyard" never fails to resound in the course of history: *it is addressed to every person who comes into this world.... You go too.* The call is a concern not only of pastors, clergy, and men and women religious. The call is addressed to everyone: lay people as well are personally called by the Lord from whom they receive a mission on behalf of the Church and the world.

—*Christifideles Laici*, December 30, 1988

Mary is the radiant sign and inviting model of the moral life. . . . Mary lived and exercised her freedom precisely by giving herself to God and accepting God's gift within herself. . . . By the gift of herself, Mary entered fully into the plan of God who gives himself to the world. By accepting and pondering in her heart events which she did not always understand, she became the model of all those who hear the word of God and keep it, and merited the title of "Seat of Wisdom." This Wisdom is Jesus Christ himself, the Eternal Word of God, who perfectly reveals and accomplishes the will of the Father. Mary invites everyone to accept this Wisdom. To us too she addresses the command she gave to the servants at Cana in Galilee during the marriage feast: "Do whatever he tells you."

—*Veritatis Splendor*, August 6, 1993

Pope John Paul II prays before a statue of the Covadonga Virgin Mary in the Asturias region of Spain. The Asturian word "Covadonga" comes from the Latin *Cova dominica*, which means "Cavern of the Lady." It is believed that the Blessed Virgin appeared there to a small Christian army and, through her intervention, the army won its first victory against invaders. (August 21, 1989)

The Pope waves to the crowd gathered for the outdoor Mass celebrated at Baltimore's Camden Yards.
This was the second visit by the pontiff; the first was in 1976 when, as Karol Cardinal Wojtyla, Archbishop
of Krakow, he visited the United States to attend the Eucharistic Congress in Philadelphia.
(Maryland, United States; October 8, 1995)

THE WORD OF GOD IS NOT ADDRESSED TO ANY ONE
PEOPLE OR TO ANY ONE PERIOD OF HISTORY. . . .
TRUTH CAN NEVER BE CONFINED TO TIME AND
CULTURE; IN HISTORY IT IS KNOWN,
BUT IT ALSO REACHES BEYOND HISTORY.

—*Fides et Ratio*, September 14, 1998

The word of God is addressed to all people,
in every age and in every part of the world.

—Fides et Ratio, September 14, 1998

On a visit to Mt. Hagen, New Guinea, the Holy Father greets Papua New Guinea Highland natives.
He met hundreds of warriors and nearly 200,000 attended the Mass that he celebrated on this trip. (May 8, 1984)

The Pope lights a candle at an interfaith ecumenical service at
St. Paul's Anglican Church in Melbourne, Australia. (November 27, 1986)

Holiness, whether ascribed to popes well known to history or to humble lay and religious figures, from one continent to another of the globe, has emerged more clearly as the dimension which expresses best the mystery of the Church. Holiness, a message that convinces without the need for words, is the living reflection of the face of Christ.

—*Novo Millennio Ineunte*, January 6, 2001

It is urgent to rediscover and to set forth once more the authentic reality of the Christian faith, which is not simply a set of propositions to be accepted with intellectual assent. Rather, faith is a lived knowledge of Christ, a living remembrance of his commandments, and a truth to be lived out. . . . Faith is a decision involving one's whole existence. It is an encounter, a dialogue, a communion of love and of life between the believer and Jesus Christ, the Way, and the Truth, and the Life. It entails an act of trusting abandonment to Christ, which enables us to live as he lived, in profound love of God and of our brothers and sisters.

—*Veritatis Splendor*, August 6, 1993

The Pope stands in front of Rio de Janeiro's 100-foot statue of Christ the Redeemer, which sits atop Brazil's Corcovado mountain. (July 2, 1980)

The Holy Father is seen in a contemplative mood during a visit to Miami, Florida. Upon his arrival, the Pope stated, "I come as a pilgrim, a pilgrim in the cause of justice and peace and human solidarity, striving to build up the one human family." (September 11, 1987)

The breath of the divine life, the Holy Spirit,
in its simplest and most common manner,
expresses itself and makes itself felt in prayer.
It is a beautiful and salutary thought that,
wherever people are praying in the
world, there the Holy Spirit is,
the living breath of prayer.

—Dominum et Vivificantem, May 5, 1986

Meeting the Risen One in faith is truly a light on man's journey, a light which calls one's whole life into question. On the shining face of Christ, God's truth manifests itself in a spectacular way. May we too keep our gaze upon the Lord!

—Homily at the Abbassyin Stadium of Damascus, May 6, 2001

The Pope waves to the crowd outside of the Shrine of Our Lady of Ludzmierz, where he led a group of faithful in the recitation of the rosary. This was the Holy Father's sixth of seven trips to his homeland during his pontificate. (Poland; June 7, 1997)

GOD CALLS EVERY PERSON, AND HIS VOICE MAKES ITSELF HEARD EVEN IN THE HEARTS OF CHILDREN. . . .

—Christmas Message to Children, December 15, 1994

. . . [T]he young people's joy, their hunger for the truth, their desire to be united all together in the Body of Christ, made clear to everyone that many, very many young people . . . have values and ideals which seldom make the headlines. Is it any wonder that the Pope loves you!

—Central Park, New York City, October 7, 1995

The Holy Father has always shown a great love toward children. Here he kisses a child outside of Argentina's Ukrainian Cathedral during his trip the Buenos Aires for World Youth Day. In a letter he wrote about World Youth Day, the Pope explained, "The principal objective of the Days is to make the person of Jesus the center of the faith and life of every young person so that he may be their constant point of reference and also the inspiration of every initiative and commitment for the education of the new generations." (April 10, 1987)

The Church has received the Eucharist from Christ her Lord not as one gift—however precious—among so many others, but as the gift *par excellence*, for it is the gift of himself, of his person in his sacred humanity, as well as the gift of his saving work. Nor does it remain confined to the past, since "all that Christ is—all that he did and suffered for all men—participates in the divine eternity, and so transcends all times."

—*Ecclesia de Eucharistia*, April 17, 2003

Pope John Paul II prays during Mass celebrated in front of the Poor Clares' convent in Stary Sacz, Poland. On this trip, he canonized Saint Kinga, daughter of the King of Hungary, foundress and nun of the Convent of Sacz. (June 16, 1999)

Oh Lord, who with your death and resurrection reveal the love of the Father,
we believe in You and with confidence we repeat today:
Jesus, I trust in You, have mercy on us and the entire world.

—Prayer for Divine Mercy Sunday, April 3, 2005

A not uncommon sight: the Pope leans on his staff as he prays during Mass in
New York City's Central Park. More than 125,000 people attended the Mass,
while thousands more thronged the outskirts of the Great Lawn.
(New York, United States; October 7, 1995)

HOPE

I wish to renew to you the invitation I gave to the entire Church at the
beginning of the new millennium: contemplate the face of Christ,
his dying face and the face of the risen One! "Jesus' cry on the Cross. . .
is not the cry of anguish of a man without hope, but the prayer of the Son
who offers his life to the Father in love, for the salvation of all." It is necessary
to welcome this message of hope in one's own life and to proclaim to
the world this revelation full of God's love. . . .

—Third International Convention of 'Young People to Assisi', August 9, 2003

Celebrating the new year, new millennium, and the start of
the Jubilee, the Pope watches New Year's Eve fireworks from his
balcony at the Vatican. (Italy; December 31, 1999)

No matter how many and great the obstacles
put in his way by human frailty and sin,
the Spirit, who renews the face of the earth,
makes possible the miracle of the perfect
accomplishment of the good. This renewal,
which gives the ability to do what is good,
noble, beautiful, pleasing to God and in
conformity with his will, is in some way the
flowering of the gift of mercy, which offers
liberation from the slavery of evil and gives
the strength to sin no more.

—*Veritatis Splendor*, August 6, 1993

A loving moment after the Pope delivered his homily for a Wednesday Mass. For many young Catholics, Pope John Paul II was the only pope they ever knew. His legacy of love and loyalty to Christ's teachings has surely influenced the future of the Church. (Vatican City; November 19, 2003)

The Pope blesses the crowd after a Mass celebrated at New York's Aqueduct Raceway. The event was hosted by the Knights of Columbus, more than 75,000 of whom welcomed the Holy Father to the papal Mass. (New York; October 6, 1995)

Many people have learned that falling does not mean the end of the road. In meeting the Savior they have heard his reassuring words: "My grace is sufficient for you; for my power is made perfect in weakness." Comforted, they have gotten up again and brought to the world the word of hope which comes from the cross. Today, having crossed the threshold of the new millennium, we are called to penetrate more deeply the meaning of this encounter. Our generation must pass on to future centuries the good news that we are lifted up again in Christ.

—Good Friday Meditations, April 21, 2000

[H]ope constantly gives new impulse to the commitment to justice and peace, as well as firm confidence in the possibility of building a better world. . . . No man or woman of good will can renounce the struggle to overcome evil with good. This fight can be fought effectively only with the weapons of love.

When good overcomes evil, love prevails and where love prevails, there peace prevails.

—World Day of Peace, January 1, 2005

The Holy Father greets the crowd during his vacation in Oropa, Italy. He visited the
Shrine of the Virgin of Oropa, home to a wooden statue of the Virgin that is believed
to have been carved by St. Luke the Evangelist and brought by St. Eusebius to
Piedmont in the fourth century. (July 16, 1989)

Surrounded by multitudes of the faithful in St. Peter's Square, the Pope lifts
a child into his arms. (Vatican City; April 11, 1979)

*Dear families, you too should be fearless, ever
ready to give witness to the hope that is in you,
since the Good Shepherd has put that hope in
your hearts through the Gospel. You should
be ready to follow Christ toward the pastures
of life, which he himself has prepared through
the Paschal Mystery of his Death and Resurrection.*

*Do not be afraid of the risks! God's
strength is always far more powerful
than your difficulties!*

—*Letter to Families*, February 22, 1994

When we walk with the Lord, we leave with him all our burdens, and this confers the strength to accomplish the mission he gives us. He who takes from us gives to us; he takes upon himself our weakness and gives us his strength. This is the great mystery of the life of the disciple and apostle. It is certain that Christ works with us and within us as we "put out into deeper waters," as now we must. When times are difficult and unpromising, the Lord himself urges us "to cast our nets once more." We must not disobey.

—*Ecclesia in Oceania*, November 22, 2001

Pope John Paul II celebrates the Mass of beatification of Anton Martin Slomsek in Maribor, Slovenia.
During his life, Bishop Slomsek helped preserve the Slovenian language and culture and
educate its people by building new schools, founding a newspaper, and a publishing house to publish
popular works in Slovenian. (September 19, 1999)

In preparation for the new millennium, the Holy Father inaugurated the restoration of the Sistine Chapel. Aside from its beauty, the Sistine Chapel also functions as the room in which the cardinals meet in conclave to elect a new pope. (Vatican City; December 11, 1999)

No human sin can erase the mercy of God, or prevent
him from unleashing all his triumphant power,
if we only call upon him. Indeed, sin itself makes even
more radiant the love of the Father who, in order
to ransom a slave, sacrificed his Son: his mercy
toward us is Redemption.

—*Veritatis Splendor*, August 6, 1993

IF LIFE AND DEATH ARE TO RETAIN THEIR
TRUE VALUE, THE DEPTHS OF CHRIST'S
SACRIFICE MUST BE UNDERSTOOD, AND WE
MUST UNITE OURSELVES TO THAT SACRIFICE
IF WE ARE TO HOLD FIRM.

—Good Friday Meditations, April 21, 2000

The Pope prays during a Mass for the students of Roman Universities
at St. Peter's Basilica. (December 14, 2004)

Pope John Paul II greets children during a Mass celebrated in Havana's Revolution Square. While it was not his first visit to a Communist nation, John Paul made history in 1989 as the first pope to visit the island nation of Cuba. It was also the first time a pope was welcome there since Fidel Castro rose to power in 1959. (Cuba; January 25, 1998)

I decided to ask you, dear boys and girls, to take upon yourselves the duty of praying for peace. You know this well: love and harmony build peace, hatred and violence destroy it. You instinctively turn away from hatred and are attracted by love: for this reason the Pope is certain that you will not refuse his request, but that you will join in his prayer for peace in the world with the same enthusiasm with which you pray for peace and harmony in your own families.

—Christmas Message to Children, December 15, 1994

Man always has before him the spiritual horizon of hope, thanks to the help of divine grace and with the cooperation of human freedom. It is in the saving Cross of Jesus, in the gift of the Holy Spirit, in the Sacraments which flow forth from the pierced side of the Redeemer, that believers find the grace and the strength always to keep God's holy law, even amid the gravest of hardships.

— *Veritatis Splendor*, August 6, 1993

During his first tour of Africa, the Holy Father greets an enthusiastic crowd outside of the Sacred Heart Church in Brazzaville, Congo. Pope John Paul II traveled extensively throughout Africa, seeing firsthand the country's trials, tribulations, and joys. (May 5, 1980)

[W]E ARE ENCOURAGED BY THE HOPE THAT COMES
FROM BEING LED BY THE PRESENCE OF THE RISEN
ONE AND THE INEXHAUSTIBLE POWER OF HIS SPIRIT,
ALWAYS CAPABLE OF NEW SURPRISES.

—*Novo Millennio Ineunte*, January 6, 2001

As the most traveled pontiff in history, Pope John Paul II was the first pope to
visit India twice, once in 1986 and again in 1999. Here, during his first visit, he
greets a large crowd before celebrating Mass. (1986)

LOVE

May your hearts be filled with the desire for genuine fraternity with all! By placing yourselves enthusiastically at the service of others, you will find meaning in your life, because Christian identity is not defined by opposition to others but by the ability to go out of oneself toward one's brothers and sisters. Openness to the world, with clarity and without fear, is part of the vocation of the Christian, conscious of his own identity and rooted in the religious heritage which the richness of the Church's witness expresses.

—Homily at the Abbassyin Stadium of Damascus, May 6, 2001

The Holy Father greets the faithful in St. Peter's Square. According to the Vatican, no other pope encountered as many individuals as did John Paul II. More than 17,600,000 pilgrims are estimated to have attended his Wednesday General Audiences alone. This figure leaves out special audiences and religious ceremonies, plus the millions of faithful the Pope met during pastoral visits throughout the world. (March 29, 1989)

LOVE OF NEIGHBOR SPRINGS FROM A LOVING HEART
WHICH, PRECISELY BECAUSE IT LOVES, IS READY TO LIVE
OUT THE LOFTIEST CHALLENGES.

—*Veritatis Splendor*, August 6, 1993

Donning a festive sombrero, the Pope greets the crowd in St. Peter's Square.
He had just returned from a visit to Mexico, where Mexican pilgrims gave him
the sombrero in thanksgiving for his visit. (April 11, 1979)

May forgiveness and brotherly love take root in human hearts.

May every weapon be laid down, and all hatred and violence put aside.

May everyone see in his neighbor not an enemy to be fought, but a brother to be accepted and loved,

so that we may join in building a better world.

—Lourdes, August 15, 2004

The Pope delivers his homily during a Mass celebrated on the Mall in Washington, DC.
(United States; October 7, 1979)

The Holy Father leans on the cross during the Good Friday *Via Crucis*
at Rome's ancient Colisseum. (April 13, 2001)

The cross of Christ . . . is also a radical revelation of mercy, or rather of the love that goes against what constitutes the very root of evil in the history of man: against sin and death. The cross is like a touch of eternal love upon the most painful wounds of man's earthly existence; it is the total fulfillment of the messianic program that Christ once formulated in the synagogue at Nazareth and then repeated to the messengers sent by John the Baptist. According to the words once written in the prophecy of Isaiah, this program consisted in the revelation of merciful love for the poor, the suffering and prisoners, for the blind, the oppressed and sinners.

—*Dives In Misericordia*, November 30, 1980

PEOPLE CANNOT LIVE WITHOUT LOVE. THEY ARE CALLED TO
LOVE GOD AND THEIR NEIGHBOR, BUT IN ORDER TO LOVE
PROPERLY THEY MUST BE CERTAIN THAT GOD LOVES THEM.
GOD LOVES YOU, DEAR CHILDREN! . . .
THIS LOVE MUST THEN SPREAD TO YOUR WHOLE COMMUNITY,
EVEN TO THE WHOLE WORLD, PRECISELY THROUGH YOU,
DEAR CHILDREN. LOVE WILL THEN BE ABLE TO REACH THOSE
WHO ARE MOST IN NEED OF IT, ESPECIALLY THE SUFFERING
AND THE ABANDONED. WHAT JOY IS GREATER THAN THE JOY
BROUGHT BY LOVE?

—Christmas Message to Children, December 15, 1994

Pope John Paul II greets the faithful before celebrating Mass at
St. Matthew's Cathedral in Washington, DC. (October 6, 1979)

At the start of the new millennium, Pope John Paul II took a three-day pilgrimage to visit and pray at the places specially linked to God's intervention in history. For his ninetieth foreign trip as pope, the Holy Father traveled to Egypt, becoming the first Roman Catholic pope to visit the country. Here, he is welcomed by a line of Moselm clerics. (February 24, 2000)

Sacred Scripture continually speaks to us
of an active commitment to our neighbor
and demands of us a shared responsibility
for all of humanity. This duty is not limited to
one's own family, nation or state, but extends
progressively to all humankind, since no one can
consider himself extraneous or indifferent to
the lot of another member of the human family.
No one can say that he is not responsible for the
well being of his brother or sister.

—*Centesimus Annus*, May 1, 1991

In the light of faith, solidarity seeks to go beyond itself, to take on the specifically Christian dimensions of total gratuity, forgiveness and reconciliation. One's neighbor is then not only a human being with his or her own rights and a fundamental equality with everyone else, but becomes the living image of God the Father, redeemed by the blood of Jesus Christ and placed under the permanent action of the Holy Spirit. One's neighbor must therefore be loved, even if an enemy, with the same love with which the Lord loves him or her; and for that person's sake one must be ready for sacrifice, even the ultimate one: to lay down one's life for the brethren.

—*Sollicitudo Rei Socialis*, December 30, 1987

Pope John Paul II greets the crowds of Lagos, Nigeria. During his eight-day tour of West Africa, the Holy Father celebrated many Masses, ordained priests, and met with leaders of non-Christian faiths and lay people of all ages and vocations. (February 14, 1982)

The Pope strikes a familiar pose during a beatification ceremony for sixteen
members of the faithful. (October 6, 1996)

The unity of all divided humanity is the will of God.
For this reason he sent his Son, so that by dying and rising
for us he might bestow on us the Spirit of love. On the eve
of his sacrifice on the Cross, Jesus himself prayed to the
Father for his disciples and for all those who believe in him,
that they might be one, a living communion. This is the
basis not only of the duty, but also of the responsibility
before God and his plan, which falls to those who through
Baptism become members of the Body of Christ, a Body in
which the fullness of reconciliation and communion must be
made present. How is it possible to remain divided, if we
have been "buried" through Baptism in the Lord's death, in
the very act by which God, through the death of his Son, has
broken down the walls of division?

—*Ut Unum Sint*, May 25, 1995

All the baptized are called to be God's priestly people in the image of Jesus, the High Priest; and as a priestly people, they are commissioned to reach out in mercy to all, particularly the most deprived, the most distant, the lost.

—*Ecclesia in Oceania*, November 22, 2001

On the Feast of the Baptism of Jesus, Pope John Paul II baptized twenty infants during a special ceremony in the Sistine Chapel. (January 13, 2002)

The Holy Father hugs three-year-old Monik and her baby sister Zin during a visit to
Antananarivo, Madagascar. (April 29, 1989)

THE INVITATION, "GO, SELL YOUR POSSESSIONS AND
GIVE THE MONEY TO THE POOR," AND THE PROMISE
"YOU WILL HAVE TREASURE IN HEAVEN," ARE MEANT FOR
EVERYONE, BECAUSE THEY BRING OUT THE FULL MEANING
OF THE COMMANDMENT OF LOVE FOR NEIGHBOR, JUST
AS THE INVITATION WHICH FOLLOWS, "COME, FOLLOW ME,"
IS THE NEW, SPECIFIC FORM OF THE COMMANDMENT OF
LOVE OF GOD. BOTH THE COMMANDMENTS AND JESUS'
INVITATION TO THE RICH YOUNG MAN STAND AT THE
SERVICE OF A SINGLE AND INDIVISIBLE CHARITY,
WHICH SPONTANEOUSLY TENDS TOWARD THAT
PERFECTION WHOSE MEASURE IS GOD ALONE.

—*Veritatis Splendor*, August 6, 1993

Love makes us seek what is good; love makes us better persons. It is love that prompts men and women to marry and form a family, to have children. It is love that prompts others to embrace the religious life or become priests. Love makes you reach out to others in need, whoever they are, wherever they are. Every genuine human love is a reflection of the Love that is God himself. . . .

—Central Park, New York, October 7, 1995

Pope John Paul II waves to the crowd during celebrations for Palm Sunday at
St. Peter's Basilica. The palm fronds symbolize Jesus' triumphant entry into
Jerusalem shortly before his crucifixion. (1995)

Every person of goodwill, keen to work
tirelessly to build the civilization of love,
must make this invitation his own:
offer forgiveness, receive peace.

—World Day of Peace, January 1, 1997

While in India for the first time, the Pope spent some time with Mother Teresa,
whom he later beatified. Here, they are pictured after visiting the Casa del Cuore Puro,
Mother Teresa's home for the destitute and dying in Calcutta. (February 3, 1986)

WE CANNOT PREACH CONVERSION UNLESS
WE OURSELVES ARE CONVERTED ANEW EVERY DAY.

—*Redemptoris Missio*, December 7, 1990

The Pope blesses a newly ordained priest at St. Peter's Basilica. The Holy Father frequently asked the faithful to pray for vocations to the priesthood. Pope John Paul II named 2005 the Year of the Eucharist, calling for the promotion of a worldwide network of prayer for vocations. (April 21, 2002)

More than 400,000 worshippers gathered for the World Youth Day XII at the Champ de Mars Park in Paris. That year's theme, taken from John 1:38-39, was chosen to reflect the pilgrims' search for meaning: "They said to [Jesus], 'Rabbi, where are you staying?' He said to them, 'Come, and you will see.'" The young faithful from more than 150 countries around the world responded to the invitation to "come and see" by exploring their faith through prayer, catechesis, the sacraments, and fellowship. (France; August 21, 1997)

Like Paul, the disciples of Christ face a great challenge: they are to transmit the Good News by expressing it in a manner suited to each culture, without losing its content or altering its meaning. Do not be afraid to bear witness to this joyful news among your brothers and sisters, by your word and by your whole life: God loves everyone and calls them to be one family in love, for they are all brothers and sisters!

—Homily at the Abbassyin Stadium of Damascus, May 6, 2001

Acts of love do not pass away.

—Good Friday Meditations at the Colosseum, April 21, 2000

Putting in practice his own advice that a vacation can provide time for spiritual reflection, Pope John
Paul II enjoys his annual holiday in the sleepy mountain hamlet of Les Combes in the Italian Alps.
The nature-loving Pope filled his days with leisurely strolls along mountain trails. (July 16, 2000)

A nun receives Communion during a Mass led by Pope John Paul II
in Roznava, Slovakia. Hundreds of people gathered under clear autumn skies
waving banners with messages of love and peace to greet the Holy Father.
(September 13, 2003)

[T]HE LORD RESURRECTED OFFERS AS
A GIFT HIS FORGIVING LOVE, RECONCILES AND
REOPENS THE SPIRIT TO HOPE. IT IS A LOVE
THAT CONVERTS HEARTS AND GIVES PEACE.
HOW MUCH NEED THE WORLD HAS TO
UNDERSTAND AND RECEIVE DIVINE MERCY!

—Prayer written for Divine Mercy Sunday, April 3, 2005

You young people will live most of your lives in the next Millennium. You must help the Holy Spirit to shape its social, moral and spiritual character. You must transmit your joy in being adopted sons and daughters of God through the creative power of the Holy Spirit. Do this with the help of Mary, Mother of Jesus. Cling to her Rosary, and you will never wander far from her side. The Pope asks you to do this. He knows that you will do this, and for this he loves you. . . . Do not be afraid! The power of the Holy Spirit is with you!

—Central Park, New York, October 7, 1995

Pope John Paul II greets a crowd of more than 3 million people—the largest gathering ever recorded—before celebrating Mass in Manila's Luneta Park. (Philippines; February 17, 1981)

I am happy and you should be happy too.
Do not weep. Let us pray together with joy.

—Vatican City, April 2, 2005

❖

At the end of the Jubilee Year, the Holy Father closes the
Holy Door at St. Peter's Basilica. (January 6, 2001)